Summary
of

The Color of Law
Richard Rothstein

Conversation Starters

By BookHabits

D1431305

Tips for Using BookHabits Conversation Starters:

EVERY GOOD BOOK CONTAINS A WORLD FAR DEEPER THAN the surface of its pages. The characters and their world come alive through the words on the pages, yet the characters and its world still live on. Questions herein are designed to bring us beneath the surface of the page and invite us into the world that lives on. These questions can be used to:

- Foster a deeper understanding of the book
- Promote an atmosphere of discussion for groups
- Assist in the study of the book, either individually or corporately
- Explore unseen realms of the book as never seen before

About Us:

THROUGH YEARS OF EXPERIENCE AND FIELD EXPERTISE, from newspaper featured book clubs to local library chapters, *BookHabits* can bring your book discussion to life. Host your book party as we discuss some of today's most widely read books.

Table of Contents

Introducing *The Color of Law*

*T*he Color of Law: A Forgotten History of How Our Government Segregated America* is an account of how federal housing policies in the early 20th century paved the way for segregation and prevented African Americans from owning homes and building wealth. Writing in the preface to his book, author Richard Rothstein says that America has a constitutional duty to put to right the government-sanctioned segregation it has implemented in the early part of the 20th century. The story of how this happened must be narrated. His purpose in writing *The Color of Law* is to "contemplate what we have collectively done and, on behalf of our government, accept responsibility." His central premise calls for a fundamental review of American constitutional law, and points to the Supreme Court's failure to realize the damning effects of racial segregation caused by unconstitutional acts by the government.

He begins the book in San Francisco, with the story of African American Frank Stevenson, who arrived from Louisiana to start a new life, becoming a worker for a manufacturing company. Rothstein tells how Stevenson had difficulty owning a new home and working in personally chosen jobs because he is black. He narrates how local and federal government authorities created separate communities for black migrants who were hoping to find fulfillment of their American Dream. The migrants' dream of a better life has mostly depended on the multigenerational growth of wealth, he explains. Land was owned and developed by homesteaders and passed these on to the next generation. Immigrants worked in industrial plants to support their children's college education. However, government intervention prevented many from taking part in this generational prosperity.This intervention included housing specified for blacks only, making financing unavailable for blacks so they could not build their own houses, discriminatory housing rules, and withholding protection for black families living in middle-class areas who are harassed by mobs who want them out of the neighborhood.

While white families were able to increase wealth as the price of houses rose up in the 1950s, their black counterparts, prevented from owning affordable houses, could not share in the American progress. The result --generations of black families remained in poverty and watched their families disintegrate. Rothstein writes how federal and local agencies became the machinery for racial discrimination and these were often established to supposedly promote affluence. The centuries belief that black and white Americans hold "natural" antipathy toward each other continued to influence government authorities and their decisions.

Politicians and lawmakers reinforced stereotypes to consolidate their authority. Rothstein shows how this operated across the country during the first half of the 20th century, the effects of which are still felt today in many places of the country.

The author suggests remedies to correct the injustice done. He stresses the importance of the 13th Amendment which disallows the government to practice slavery and thereby erase its legacy. He also points out that the 14th Amendment dictates equality among all American citizens. He says the Bill of Rights and the Civil War Amendments are meant to prevent popular and powerful groups to take advantage of government positions to practice their discriminatory activities. He suggests solutions but he knows that such suggestions are not acceptable to many and there is no easy fix.

The book is heavy on the weight of evidence the author presents to readers. His data which goes back to the late 19th century dispels the notion that government is a minor player in creating ghettos populated by blacks. Just about every presidential administration had a role in creating policies of de jure (government-sponsored) segregation, and his careful analyses of multiple historical documents strongly support his claims. He has a clear and meticulously detailed writing style delivered in short and straightforward chapters. Logic and conclusions are tight which make it difficult to to argue against. A dense book despite its shortness, he gives examples from current day progressive areas such as the Bay Area, New York, and Boston. The well-structured book cites policies like the New Deal, post-war highway construction, state-sanctioned violence and how all these were used to ensure segregation and poverty of generations of African-Americans. Individual stories are incorporated to illustrate real life impact of government actions. All these factors combine to convey the serious effect that government action has done. In the final chapters, Rothstein lists things that might have led to a kind of America so different from today.

The New York Times review calls *The Color of Law* powerful and disturbing. Book critics, historians, and law authorities think it is one of the rare books that will be discussed and debated for many decades. They agree that the book reveals a history of racism that Americans are blind to and compels citizens to do something about the consequences of unjust government policies.

Discussion Questions

"Get Ready to Enter a New World"

Tip: Begin with questions dealing with broader issues to ensure ample time for quality discussions. Read through all discussion questions before engaging.

question 1

Richard Rothstein blames the American government for making a caste system through discrimination of African Americans through its government acts. Do you agree that there is a caste system in the US? Why? Why not?

~ ~ ~

question 2

Rothstein further claims that these discriminatory government policies do not exist anymore but they were never corrected. The harrowing effects continue to this day. In what way do the effects of anti-black government policies endure? Have these effects debilitated black families in a serious way?

~ ~ ~

question 3

The Color of Law provides a lot of evidence to support Rothstein's claim about the US government's major responsibility in creating racial ghettos. Can you cite policies that the government had that promoted racial segregation? How do you feel about these government policies?

question 4

Rothstein uncovers racial segregation policies in every presidential administration even going back to late 19th century. What does this say about past US presidents? Do you think they intentionally promoted racial segregation?

~~~

question 5

The Color of Law, according to Rothstein, is meant to stir Americans to think about what was done to their fellow citizens and to accept responsibility for it. What do you think of this stated purpose of the book? Do you think government authorities, past and present, will acknowledge what has been done and accept responsibility for it?

~~~

question 6

While white families were able to increase wealth as the price of houses rose up in the 1950s, their black counterparts, prevented from owning affordable houses, could not share in the American progress. This resulted to generations of black families remaining in poverty as they watched their families disintegrate. Does this change your view of poor blacks? Do you believe in the claim that poverty among African Americans is a result of their lack of determination and ambition?

~~~

question 7

According to Rothstein, the poverty suffered by blacks is directly caused by government's non-action. It did not implement the basic rights constitutionally mandated for African Americans. Are the evidence cited by Rothstein convincing? How does it change your view of the government, the Constitution and democracy?

~~~

~~~

question 8

The book is heavy on the weight of evidence the author presents to readers. His data dispels the notion government is a minor player in creating ghettos populated by blacks. Do you think the book is successful in presenting its argument? Do the evidence make the book convincing?

~~~

question 9

Rothstein has a clear and meticulously detailed writing style delivered in short and straightforward chapters. Do you like the way the author wrote the book? Does he make it easy for you to understand technical terms about law, real estate, and urban planning?

~~~

question 10

. Individual stories are incorporated in the book to illustrate real life impact of government actions. How do individual stories affect the book's overall narrative? Do the stories help you understand the situation of African Americans who have a hard time accumulating wealth? In what way?

~~~

~~~

question 11

Rothstein begins the book in San Francisco, with the story of African American Frank Stevenson, who arrived from Louisiana and found work in the manufacturing industry. Rothstein tells how Stevenson is blocked from owning a new home and certain jobs because he is black. Why do you think Rothstein opens the book with this story? What is the purpose of the story in relation to the whole book?

~~~

~~~

question 12

Government intervention included racialized public housing and zoning, denial of government-supported financing for black Americans, implementation of discriminatory housing covenants, and allowing private mobs to drive African-Americans out of middle-class neighborhoods. How do you feel about the government doing such actions? Do you think this is the role of governments with regard to its citizens?

~~~

question 13

The author proposes remedies to correct the injustice done. He argues that the 13th Amendment requires the government to prohibit slavery and remove its legacy from the nation. He also points out the 14th Amendment's mandate of equality under the law. Why do you think the segregation happened despite the constitutional amendments protecting the rights of African Americans?

~~~

question 14

. Rothstein demonstrates that the government and courts upheld racist policies. This has led to violent situations like those that happened in Ferguson, Baltimore, Charleston, and Chicago. Do you think governments and courts could have prevented violence from erupting long before they actually happened? In what way?

~~~

question 15

The impact of segregation has affected generations of African-Americans whose rights were denied them -- to live where they wanted to live, and send their children to schools where they thought best. Do you think the government can still remedy the situation? How do you think the government should correct its mistakes?

~~~

~~~

question 16

The New York Times review says the book provides lots of evidence to reveal the government policies that led to segregation. This includes acts done by presidential administrations.Do you think the weight of evidence presented is a strength of the book? Can you imagine the book without the evidence presented?

~~~

question 17

The Goodreads review says the violence and unrest that recently plagued Ferguson, Baltimore, and Minneapolis are a result of segregation policies in the earlier eras. Do you agree with the review? Do you think the unrest today is related to past policies of the government?

question 18

The American Conservative says *The Color of Law* should cause concerned citizens to initiate moves that will solve urban problems, poverty and race issues. The review suggests that Conservatives take the book seriously. Do you think the book will spur supporters of the Constitution and those in government and free market to do something about the effects of segregation? Can this lead to revolutionary actions?

question 19

The Economic Policy Institute says *The Color of Law* is about the whole of America, including both red and blue states. It does not address just a particular group of Americans, but everyone, whether they are liberal or reactionary. Do you think racism is not limited to the South? Is it a mistaken myth that the Southerners are racists and the Northerners are not?

~~~

question 20

Ira Katznelson, author of the Bancroft Prize–winning *Fear Itself*, says *The Color of Law* reveals why segregation continues and even persisted even after the Civil Rights era. Do you think segregation has deepened in the post-civil rights era? Are black Americans still being treated like slaves today?

~~~

Introducing the Author

Richard Rothstein works with the Thurgood Marshall Institute of the NAACP Legal Defense Fund as fellow. He also works with the Economic Policy Institute as research associate, and with the Haas Institute at the University of California (Berkeley) as fellow. Aside from his latest book *The Color of Law,* he has also authored *Grading Education: Getting Accountability Right* (2008); *Class and Schools: Using Social, Economic and Educational Reform to Close the Black-White Achievement Gap* (2004); and *The Way We Were? Myths and Realities of America's Student Achievement* (1998). He co-authored the two recent books *Charter School Dust-Up: Examining the Evidence on Enrollment and Achievement* (2005); and *All Else Equal: Are Public and Private Schools Different?* (2003). Rothstein used to be a senior fellow at the Berkeley's law school's Chief Justice Earl Warren Institute on Law and Social Policy. The institute closed in 2015.

His areas of expertise include civil rights, desegregation, education, educational equity, race and education, and racial inequality. A former columnist for the New York Times Rothstein has spent years documenting the evidence that government promoted discriminatory practices in residential housing. He says segregation is a government creation. If people understand this, then creating a remedial action is possible. Though segregation practices are long gone, the effects remain. When talking about solutions, he thinks desegregating housing today will not fix the problem right away. Desegregating suburbs limited to whites only are no longer affordable to many African Americans, but they were affordable to them when they were first built. African American wealth today is about seven percent of white wealth. He explains that the enormous difference between white and African American wealth today "is almost entirely attributable to the federal unconstitutional housing policy of the mid-20th century." He thinks that presidential administrations will not be able to correct the situation unless there is a consensus that there is de jure or government-sanctioned segregation. His book is meant to assist in the development of such consensus along with other authors who wrote on the subject.

Residential segregation is entrenched and exacerbates serious political, social and economic problems. Rothstein further explains that hostile and fatal confrontations between police and African American youth could be prevented if the poorest young people were not concentrated in areas that prevent them from participating in meaningful activities. These unhealthy neighborhoods do not provide good jobs, well-provided schools, and transportation to better opportunities. Rothstein explains how these segregated neighborhoods trap the most disadvantaged young black men . African American children are more likely to remain poor if they live in these segregated areas. "We've done little to desegregate neighborhoods," he says. On the other hand, integrated neighborhoods with a big middle class population have a police force who act as public servants, not as occupying forces, which is why violence and crime are not as common.

In his book *Class and Schools,* Rothstein echoes the same concern for social policies that close the gap between advantaged whites and the disadvantaged poor including African Americans.

Racial and income gaps play a role in children's school performance and achievement, he says, and a solution to this is addressing the inequalities in American life.

Fireside Questions

"What would you do?"

Tip: These questions can be a fun exercise as it spurs creativity among the readers by allowing alternate scene endings and "if this was you" questions.

question 21

. Richard Rothstein is a fellow at the Thurgood Marshall Institute of the NAACP Legal Defense Fund. He is also a research associate of the Economic Policy Institute, and a fellow at the Haas Institute at the University of California (Berkeley). Do you think his being a researcher is instrumental to his writing? Could he have written his books if he is not with a university and policy institute?

~~~

question 22

. Aside from *The Color of Law,* he has also authored and co-authored other books. Are there any the common factors among his books? Can you say what kind of person he is based on his books?

~~~

~~~

question 23

He explains that the enormous difference between white and African American wealth today "is almost entirely attributable to the federal unconstitutional housing policy of the mid-20th century." Have you thought of how your family's wealth became possible through the support of government policies on housing? Were these policies helpful?

~~~

~~~

question 24

Rothstein explains that hostile and violent encounters between black youth and the police could be prevented if the neighborhoods they live in are provided with good jobs, quality schools, and access to better opportunities. Do you agree with him? Does this give you a better understanding of black poverty?

~~~

~~~

question 25

African American children are more likely to remain poor if they live in segregated neighborhoods, according to Rothstein. He claims that the government and citizens in power have not done much to solve poor, segregated communities. Do you think there is something you can do to desegregate neighborhoods? In what way?

~~~

question 26

Rothstein argues that the recent incidents of violence and mayhem in black-populated areas in America are proof that the segeragation policies in earlier eras have caused racial-related unrest to fester. If the violence did not erupt in these areas, do you think Rothstein would have written the book? Do you think the unrest is the only reason why he wrote the book?

question 27

He reveals that segregation happened even during presidential administrations that were thought of as liberal. If at least one president actively opposed the racial segregation being implemented by the government, do you think black history would have changed? If yes, in what way?

question 28

The author has solutions to correct the injustice done to generations of African Americans. He cites the 13th Amendment and the 14th Amendment as proof that African Americans have the right to create a better life. If he did not use the Constitution as basis for his proposal that government correct its racist acts, do you think his argument will be listened to? Is the Constitution the only reason why racism should be corrected

question 29

Rothstein begins the book in San Francisco, with the story of African American Frank Stevenson, who arrived from Louisiana, intending to work and start a new life . Rothstein tells how Stevenson could not own a new home and find a job he likes because he is black. If the author opened the book with a story of racism in the South instead of racism in San Francisco, do you think it would be an equally arresting opening? Why? Why not?

question 30

Rothstein has a clear and meticulously detailed writing style delivered in short and straightforward chapters. If he wrote in a literary style, do you think the book would be as powerful and appealing to its readers?

Quiz Questions

"Ready to Announce the Winners?"

Tip: Create a leaderboard and track scores to see who gets the most correct answers. Winners required. Prizes optional.

quiz question 1

. *The Color of Law* by Richard Rothstein is an account of how federal housing policies in the early _____ century paved the way for segregation and prevented African Americans from owning homes and building wealth.

quiz question 2

His central premise demands that a review be made of the Constitution , and points to the failure of the _____ to understand the effects of segregation and the fact that it is a consequence of unconstitutional acts by the government.

quiz question 3

He begins the book in _____, with the story of African American Frank Stevenson, who arrived from Louisiana and found work in the manufacturing industry. Rothstein tells how Stevenson is blocked from owning a new home and certain jobs because he is black.

~~~

~~~

quiz question 4

True or False: Rothstein describes how local and federal authorities created integrated neighborhoods as black migrants came to California hoping to find fulfillment of their American Dream.

~~~

quiz question 5

True or False: Government intervention included racialized public housing and zoning, denial of government-supported financing for black Americans, implementation of discriminatory housing covenants, and allowing private mobs to drive African-Americans out of middle-class neighborhoods.

~~~

quiz question 6

True or False: Rothstein argues that the 13th Amendment requires the government to prohibit slavery and remove its legacy from the nation.

~ ~ ~

~~~

quiz question 7

True or False: Some, not all, presidential administrations played a role in creating policies of de jure (government-sponsored) segregation. Rothstein's careful analyses of multiple historical documents strongly support his claims.

~~~

~~~

quiz question 8

Rothstein is a _____ of the Economic Policy Institute.

~~~

quiz question 9

He says police act as _____, not as occupying forces, when they are in integrated neighborhoods with a big middle class population.

~ ~ ~

~~~

quiz question 10

True or False: Rothstein explains how segregated neighborhoods trap the most disadvantaged young black men . They don't have adequate access to good jobs or education, and are guarded by police.

~~~

quiz question 11

True or False: In his book *Class and Schools,* Rothstein echoes the same concern for social policies that close the gap between advantaged whites and the disadvantaged poor including African Americans.

quiz question 12

True or False: He explains that the enormous difference between white and African American wealth today "is partly attributable to the federal unconstitutional housing policy of the mid-20th century."

~ ~ ~

Quiz Answers

1. 20th
2. Supreme Court
3. San Francisco
4. False
5. True
6. True
7. False
8. research associate
9. public servants
10. True
11. True
12. False

Ways to Continue Your Reading

EVERY month, our team runs through a wide selection of books to pick the best titles for readers and reading groups, and promotes these titles to our thousands of readers – sometimes with free downloads, sale dates, and additional brochures.

If you have not yet read the original work or would like to read it again, get the book here.

Want to register yourself or a book group? It's free and takes 1-click.

Register here.

On the Next Page...

Please write us your reviews! Any length would be fine but we'd appreciate hearing you more! We'd be SO grateful.

Till next time,

BookHabits

"Loving Books is Actually a Habit"

CPSIA information can be obtained
at www.ICGtesting.com
Printed in the USA
LVHW051227290620
659185LV00002B/184

9 781389 423000